Brain Fever

ALSO BY KIMIKO HAHN

Toxic Flora

The Narrow Road to the Interior

The Artist's Daughter

Mosquito and Ant

Volatile

The Unbearable Heart

Earshot

Air Pocket

Brain Fever

POEMS

Kimiko Hahn

W. W. Norton & Company

NEW YORK | LONDON

For information about permission to reproduce selections from this book,
write to Permissions, W. W. Norton & Company, Inc.,
500 Fifth Avenue, New York, NY 10110

For information about special discounts for bulk purchases, please contact
W. W. Norton Special Sales at specialsales@wwnorton.com or 800-233-4830

Manufacturing by Courier Westford
Book design by Fearn Cutler de Vicq
Production manager: Devon Zahn

Library of Congress Cataloging-in-Publication Data

Hahn, Kimiko, 1955–
[Poems. Selections]
Brain fever : poems / Kimiko Hahn. — First edition.
pages ; cm
Includes bibliographical references.
ISBN 978-0-393-24335-2 (hardcover)
I. Title.
PS3558.A32357A6 2014
811'.54—dc23

2014013659

W. W. Norton & Company, Inc., 500 Fifth Avenue, New York, NY 10110
www.wwnorton.com

W. W. Norton & Company Ltd., Castle House,
75/76 Wells Street, London W1T 3QT

1 2 3 4 5 6 7 8 9 0

for Tomie

Contents

Brain Fever

[Things that make one's stomach churn]

> the reverse side of a brocade
> the inside of a cat's ear
> newborn mice, hairless and pink, squirming from their nest
> the seam of an as-yet-unlined leather robe
> a dingy dark recess
> a homely woman tending to her sizable brood
> a woman who has been sick for a spell—she must strike her
>   lover, especially if he is not that caring towards her, as
>   distasteful

[Kimiko's Clipping Morgue: BRAIN file]

BRAIN: *"In Pursuit of a Mind Map, Slice by Slice"*

BRAIN *behavior: see* SHAME, DISTRUST, OCD/ *neurotransmitters,* Rapunzel syndrome, *etc.*

BRAIN *misc.: "Flame First, Think Later: New Clues to E-Mail Misbehavior"*; sealed manila envelope labeled *her vitals*

BRAIN *memory: "Memory Implant Gives Rats Sharper Recollection"; "No Memory, but He Filled In the Blanks"; "Researchers Create Artificial Memories in the Brain of a Fruitfly"*; photo of Rei tottering on sandy path as Miya runs toward me, the camera—scribbled on back, *girls' first summer on Fire Island*

BRAIN PAN: *[empty]*

BRAIN DRAIN: *[empty]*

BRAIN *and head syn.: attic, bean, belfry, brain box, conk, dome, noddle, noodle, gray matter*

BRAIN dreams (see DREAM THEORY)

BAIN [sic], origin Old English bana, thing causing poison (see DUPLICITY)

[file without label]: Spirit Photograph Exhibit/admit two, lavender lace thong, two flattened Chinese handcuffs

BRAIN fever: . . . 2. a medical condition where a part of the brain becomes inflamed and causes symptoms that present as fever. The terminology is dated, and is encountered most often in Victorian literature, where it typically describes an illness brought about by a severe emotional upset.

BRAIN poetry: Blake, "Mad Song"; Dickinson, "I felt a Funeral, in my Brain"; Poe, "The Haunted Palace"; Jeffers, "Apology for Bad Dreams"; Anne Sexton, "Angel of Flight and Sleigh Bells";

BRAIN Shakespeare: "these paper bullets of the brain," "In this distracted globe," "dagger of the mind," "Raze out the written troubles of the brain," "memory, the warder of the brain."

BRAIN split (see CONSCIOUSNESS, see WIFE)

consciousness

Alarm

Before doctors learn how it is that the brain's lights turn on,
they may have to know a lot more about what's happening
when the lights are off.

—BENEDICT CAREY

In her dark she surveys empty: the vanity
from the in-laws' Bronx apartment,

the brooch from a lover,
loafers by a coat tree, trench coat,

the husband's profile, an alarm

for news and forecast. Here
                          she appraises fidelity
before the light violates.

Wake

Waking: Canadian geese take flight from pond to field,

a school bus idles across the road, my husband
fetches wood and lights a fire—even before

I hear the electric toothbrush then his shower.
A wanton beeping, his cell. Yes?

Or am I still under

a B&B comforter or on some gurney—?
Does a flicker matter to anyone but the attendant

who watches for awake in muted fluorescence?

Figure

Here is the interior without sense:
no grizzled dog woofing in sleep,

no steam hissing from a radiator
or words from next door. Or *yes,*

murmurs through the wall abruptly

concrete, what makes the birthing room pronounced:
forfeiting grays

from mother's pulse
to wattage. The infant faces such passage

before figuring out significance.

The What-Have-You

Modern scientists . . . also have analyzed what happens in the brain when people suddenly become aware of an object that was hidden in plain sight.

— BENEDICT CAREY

For some, awareness amounts to
banning a same-sex rendezvous

in mosh pit or on carousel.
That is, there is no Awareness.

Not for Chanel No. what-have-you.

Not for fracking or mean-girl-ing.
(Maybe for jilting.)

Even for the blue whale
the scant Awareness is mainly green.

As well, in the corner of a continent—

obstetric fistula, symptomatic of what
someone has referred to as holocaust.

Porch Light

Barley. Poppy. Then pomegranate.
Now front porch light.

There's no longer sensation without the one

once cradled in tissue, swaddled in blood—
feeling her hiccup inside the inside.

Turn the pages of a calendar
to retrieve one's daughter

from his underground vow.

I must unlock the door, leave it ajar,
since by degrees

the son-in-law rations my weather.

Skull

Little oxygen? No light? No water?
Certainly no fragrant hands brushing aside one's hair.

No novel read until the head nods.
Or yes—the story is how Snow White fled

to serve seven dwarfs who, in the end,
laid her out in a glass coffin

while they read to her in kind.
Beware the apple, bodice, comb,

the absent father and cannibal mother.

Beware the predestined ever-after
that stays behind in a room of bone.

The Dream of a Little Occupied Japan Doll

Among the hundred porcelain figurines,
the first one—with slanted eyes, fat cheeks,

queue (though that's Chinese), and Chinese bonnet—
is my favorite. Among all those in pajamas

or gowns or the two in kimono,
the first is my favorite. Of those with rickshaw,

tambourine, or parasol and fan—
I keep on my desk the first one

though she—or he—is not doing a darn thing.
Here in sleep, rivalry is reserved.

And as dreams "tune the mind for conscious awareness"
perhaps this favoritism suggests

I've quit hoarding and now collect myself.

For Alice and Laurie

Tiny Wheels

Before sunup, the bar below cranks the gate down
and the neighbor's toddler starts up:

come here, not you, I won't, da da, don't go

Later, in the real morning with real light,
you scatter the Sunday paper over our comforter

to bolster discomfort. Then again from next door
I hear a matchbox car

racing up and down the shared-wall. Yes, tiny wheels
from a boy's self-absorbed spell.

Or maybe I sense the subway roaring below the
pavement.

Or the residue of shock, seismic and illicit—

Safe

*The deeper that investigators dig [for the origin of
consciousness], the more hidden chambers they find.*
                                                    —BENEDICT CAREY

Inside the ant farm's plastic pane
the sandy routes disclose rooms to store

a Harley retirement pin left by Grandpa Aaron,
two wedding rings she cannot pawn or wear,

a lacquer comb, a baby's incisor
and in her wall safe, intercepted correspondence

between husband and sycophant.
She frantically revisits that mail

to grasp their phrase: *harmless fun*—

to restore the unsafe,
            so familiar in the gritty tunnel on display.

Gag

*. . . more than enjoying company, [the brain] needs
interactions to develop, to regulate mood, to solve problems,
to respond to threats.*
—BENEDICT CAREY

When my therapist asks, "Why rent a beach house
if you despise visitors?" I realize

I despise my therapist
even if she needles until I confess

I can't stomach a vacation
with dear ones since those dear ones

pack arsenic as cure-all,
a sword for swallowing

and a gag for spilling family dirt—

until I survey her throbbing beige office and quit.

A Bowl of Spaghetti

"To find a connectome, or the mental makeup of a
    person,"
researchers experimented with the neurons of a worm

then upgraded to mouse hoping to
"unravel the millions of miles of wires in the [human]
    brain"

that they liken to "untangling a bowl of spaghetti"

of which I have an old photo: Rei in her high chair
    intently
picking out each strand to mash in her mouth.

Was she two? Was that sailor dress from Mother?
Did I cook that sauce from scratch? If so, there was a
    carrot in the pot,

as Mother instructed and I'll never forget
                                no matter which strand
determines ardor as a daughter's verdict.

Turns of Mind

Five thousand black birds fall from the sky—

not mid-fairytale but *News at Six*. Once established
neither army test nor pesticide is at fault,

the mind races for causative agents in case we're next.

Ah. Did the flock soar into some Invisible Divide
from another Dimension à la *The Twilight Zone?*

Did the flock cross an exacting God? A ranger suggests
coincident fireworks

flushed the birds at such speed that they crashed into

buildings and power lines and in fact
                                    necropsies do disclose

"blunt force trauma to brain and breast."
Even so, since pyrotechnics are not sufficiently ominous

the blogosphere keeps alive a quest for the fabulous.

dream

The Dream of Parsnips

Do I wish for a box of cigars—or dynamite?
Do I wish for the sudden squirming of earthworms?

Do I wish for the dense smell in Grandma Ida's dining
    room
or some prix fixe? Do I wish for

the standing-outside-his-lit-office-window-at-two-in-
    the-morning
as only a sophomore can stand . . . or for

the husband to scrap the skank?
Or perhaps for the researcher herself who believes:

"dreaming is not a parallel state but consciousness itself,

in the absence of the senses' input"?
Considering various explanatory projects,

I *do* wish that wishing would process
whatever calls up an object so white and duplicitous.

The Dream of Bubbles

The unborn "may be 'seeing' something
long before the eyes ever open"—seeing that later

makes sense of Mr. Bubble or bubbly with an alum
and why I can't visit the museum's

giant squid and whale diorama. Also

the reason I can't open my eyes in pond or pool

to witness the weight of loan.
And why I can't bear the chatter of toddlers

as if sinking to the bottom of a basin. Can I burst
through the transparent?

After all, "the developing brain draws on innate,

biological models of space and time."
Fear blue, fear green, stay clear of aquamarine.

The Dream of a Pillow

Zealous mother or breast,
zealous marshmallow, zealous feathers.

Although the neuroscientist

does not declare, *so what*—
she does believe the brain

observes prop and scene
in a lucid watchfulness

which may play out in proverb or verse
or be utterly meaningless.

Zealous codeine. Zealous noose.

The Dream of a Letter Opener
in the Shape of a Mermaid

Tell me which ocean is warmest,

tell me which shore is closest,
tell me which ship tosses trash and which plays a waltz

and how many bottles you've collected
containing messages from shipwrecks.

Is this figure playing in my mind
an unconscious desire or archetypal theme

or are these explanations merely "predetermined ideas,"

assumptions made theory——?
Not wishing to jam the round peg in that square

I also don't wish to submit to
    gastrointestinal or neurological pleasures:
tell me about the sister in a glass case,

a monkey's body glued to that of a fish.

The Dream of Knife, Fork, and Spoon

I can't recall where to set the knife and spoon.
I can't recall which side to place the napkin

or which bread plate belongs to me. Or
how to engage in benign chatter.

I can't recall when more than one fork—
which to use first. Or what to make of a bowl of water.

I can't see the place cards or recall any names.
The humiliation is impressive. The scorn.

No matter how much my brain "revises" the dinner

to see if the host was a family member—
I can't recall which dish ran away with which spoon.

For Jill

The Dream of *Shōji*

How to say *milk*? How to say *sand, snow, sow,*

linen, cloud, cocoon, or *albino*?
How to say *page* or *canvas* or *rice balls*?

Trying to recall Japanese, I blank out:

it's clear I know *forgetting*. Mother, tell me
what to call that paper screen that slides the interior in?

The Dream of a Lacquer Box

I wish I knew the contents and I wish the contents
Japanese—

like hairpins made of tortoiseshell or bone
though my braid was lopped off long ago,

like overpowering pine incense
or a talisman from a Kyoto shrine,

like a Hello Kitty diary-lock-and-key,
Hello Kitty stickers or candies,

a netsuke in the shape of a squid,
ticket stubs from *A Double Suicide*—

or am I wishing for mother? searching for sister?
just hoping to give something Japanese to my daughters?

then again, people can read anything into dreams

and I do as well. I wish I possessed my mother's
black lacquer box though in my dream it was red,

though I wish my heart were cóntent.

The Dream of a Fire Engine

Without the sun filtering through closed eyelids,
without the siren along the service road,

without Grandpa's ginger-colored hair,
Mother's lipstick, Daughter's manicure,

firecrackers, a monkey's ass, a cherry, Rei's lost elephant,
without past tense, deficit or communist,

without Mao's favorite novel about a chamber,
or the character seeing her own chopped-off feet dancing
    in fairy slippers,

or the siren with a prof at a hot-sheet-motel—

the scientist of sleep has claimed
that without warm blood a creature cannot dream.

The Terrible-Headed-Lizard-from-the-Orient

Far from my grade school *The Golden Treasury of Natural
    History*
with its illustration of the ancient reptile, protorosaur,

I see that paleontologists have unearthed more fossils.
Now they realize that those monstrous necks—

twice as long as their three-foot trunks—
might've been functional: that two hundred million
    years ago

hunting in ancient seas was tough
since any quick movement pushed their prey off.

Turtles and fish solved this same dilemma
with suction feeding—that is, by rapidly expanding the
    mouth cavity—

and apparently so did the Terrible-Headed-Lizard-from-
    the-Orient

which presents a greater illustration of nightmare than I
    even knew,
since their necks evolved into a giant suction tube, you.

Ode to Home

Snails are such a pick-me-up

and Darwin thought so too
though he was "greatly perplexed"

by the existence of the Roman land snail:
how could a creature so readily killed by salt

contrive to populate oceanic islands?
In his room he submerged them in seawater

until egg and snail survived these "long baths"—

surmising that the lowly Helix Pomatia
must have been "transported to islands

by adhering to driftwood or the feet of birds."
I, too, contrive to lug a house on my shoulders

since it finally protects against origin.

time

"A French explorer named Michel Siffre lived in a cave for two months, cut off from [daily] rhythms [and emerged] convinced that he had been isolated for only 25 days."

Dust in nostrils
Dust in the dark
Dank clothes, dank *omamori*, moist walls, sludge
    underfoot—
Sneakers
Tubers?
The word *tubers* and the thought of tubers
Hunger pangs—O Twinkies! O Nachos! O Snickers!
Sneakers
(never finished that class on Plato when I holed up at a
    boyfriend's—only to find him hollow)
Dust in hair, under fingernails
Dank harness
(I loved Jarrell's *Bat Poet* because I had no friends
    either—)
Bats
My sister's watch, no longer coherent

"[Some psychologists say] the findings support the philosopher Martin Heidegger's observation that time 'persists merely as a consequence of the events taking place in it.'"

Water breaks
Rain on the windshield during Braxton-Hicks
Caesarean
Commencement
Standing in line for theater tickets to see *Metamorphosis*
Mother is always nearby with things. Pillows. Hot-water bottle.
  She loves her infant granddaughter more than she loves
  anyone, even me. And I love that.
Clutching a baby to one hip, a ladle in the other hand.
Do you recall me cooking? I can barely recall what I threw
  together. Yet you girls have grown to be so striking—
Standing in line at 4 a.m. to get her into the good
  kindergarten—that was their father—
Standing at the checkout, a child in the cart sobbing for
  bubble gum
Commencement. The Gulf.
A girl! A girl!
Commencement
Crowning

"But the way [the brain] fixes the relative timing of events depends on memory, the new study found."

Dendrite, "the branching process of a neuron that conducts impulses toward the cell." From Gk, *pertaining to a tree.*
Pine
Pine coffin—*Mama, Mama*—
Fir
Fur
A green cashmere sweater he purchased for her so she wouldn't leave. She stayed and they fucked in every room of his parents' house. Just not on the mahogany double.
Leaf through the novel, even the electronic version. Snowy screen. Snowball, snowbank, snowstorm. Electrical storm.
From the electric rice-cooker, a kind of gruel. Salty. Maybe a little *furikake.* Obviously not sled or madeleine. Snow peas.
Maybe a storage pod.
Cartons of childhood possessions—some no longer viable.
(The marriage locked in chests—what does that even mean—)
(No longer *zoetic*)
A videotape of girls twirling on the Oriental.

"Yet the sensation of passing time can be very different. Dr. Zauberman said, 'depending on what you think about, and how.'"

Tweezing eyebrows and thinking about refinancing the
    mortgage
Tweezing eyebrows and mulling over a daughter's
    curfew
Baking biscuits and not thinking (was I sixteen?)
While tweezing, I think to use the pressure cooker for
    the New Year's *sekihan*.
Riding in a train to visit my sister and recalling how I
    told her to *be quiet* every night of our childhood (*I'm*
    so sorry)
Sorrow
As her father drove her to flute lessons she kept talking
    so he wouldn't ask what she was up to.
Tweezing eyebrows while fuming over the lice outbreak
Fuck it. Five minutes left of the test, she filled in the rest
    of the bubbles.
Riding in the train to see him, the heat blasting the seat
    and the vibration arousing—
He loved researching at the Forty-second Street Library:
    the rolls of microfilm on penny dreadfuls.

Rebooting

Googling *Syria.*

Tweezing, I recall last night: our pulses flashed in the
slant of streetlight across the bed.

The Solitary Adelie

She peers into reticent waters near Hut Point
and if you've ever arranged a blind date

at a designated window in the Central Park Zoo
you know what she wants. If you've taken your little girl

to the aquarium on Lake Michigan, ditto.
Or found yourself on Cape Adare, solitary, too—

ditto. After all, she simply seeks affirmation beneath that
    glaze:

is it too much to hope for a squid this evening?
Not at all. After which, I venture, an introvert could
    well attend

to the brouhaha of a million.

The Secret Lives of Planets

LINES LIFTED FROM "NOW IN SIGHT: FAR-OFF PLANETS,"

DENNIS OVERBYE

whether the bodies are really planets or failed stars—
the first team spied a pair of dots about four billion miles out—
telescope mirrors are jiggled and warped—

"Every extrasolar planet detected so far has been a wobble"—
swaddled in large disks of dust, the raw material of worlds—
the bodies are really planets or failed stars—

"Kepler himself would recognize [how they follow] his laws of
*   orbital motion"—*
fuzzy dots moving slightly around from exposure to exposure—
jiggled and warped—

three planets circle a star known as HR 8799 in constellation
*   Pegasus—*
The problem seeing other planets is picking them from the glare
*   of parent stars—*
or failed stars—

giant planets in the outer reaches, [leave] plenty of room
for smaller ones to lurk undetected in the warmer inner regions—
whether parents are really failed stars—
telescopic, mirrored and warped—

puzzles

Giraffes

After skimming the Sunday *Times*, Dad turned to the
    back of the magazine
and tore out the crossword puzzle for his mother in
    Wisconsin—

as routine as my calligraphy class on Saturdays, flute
    practice
exactly twenty minutes on school nights

and astringent twice a day. I loved the idea of puzzles
but never tried my hand as problem-solving rubbed up
    against rivalry—

red velvet cake, red velvet dress, trilling—

because nothing was never enough and yet
more than a small rectangular lawn and the pulsing
    marsh beyond.

A puzzle might've been escape enough. A maze—instead
    of crossword?

No, cross *words* were our puzzles, after all. Although my
   sister and I adored
jigsaw pieces. Five hundred. A zoo, I think. Giraffes,
   absolutely.

Fiero

The gamer is drawn into "flow"—
a state of focus for athlete, musician

and a small girl dog-paddling to Grandpa Okuno—
because the computer offers continual encouragement

over bazooka or crossbow

or metallic-pink laser. The undead, no doubt.
Here, anyone can fail over and over

                            and persist:

"[the profound transformation] we can learn from
    games is
how to turn the sense that one has 'failed'

into the sense that she 'hasn't succeeded yet.'" Oh, *fierce*
    pride!

Oh, kanji and swan dive!
Oh, lecturing on Emily Dickinson year after year to
    undergrads!

Riddle

Here you are: *snow-*, *cup-*, *floor-*, *water-*. Go.

Give up? A hint: *-room.*
Another hint: the last two are coincident with current

monopoly-capitalist operations. Give up?
Also a synonym for *ennui.*

Not yet?

And speaking of current events, there's *Abu Ghraib.*
Oh, no. That was truncheon, wire, and phosphorescent
    tube.

Give up?

Mapping

Mother loved to unfold and smooth out
the red- and black-veined sheet on her lap,

revealing shortcuts
so she and Dad could scour every flea market and
    collectibles shop

for Occupied Japan figurines—
a dedicated search but open for a find

as if each grid were one of a zillion slivers of the brain,
sliced, dyed, set on silicon,

abruptly illuminating where consciousness abides.

Madagascan Hissing Cockroaches

The females hang out and the males fight to make the
 scene—
same ol' same ol' but with a new research twist:

that a medium-sized guy is the most ferocious

(ramming heads, flipping the adversary, whacking, and
 so on)
because he benefits most from aggressive behavior. But

did the girls really just hang around for some action?
I hate that.

the teenage brain

Dopamine : I'm crossing the street.
There's a truck approaching me and . . . oh, look at
the cute doggy!

footfall as she nears her vestibule,
hurricane, tsunami, earthquake, wildfire, volcanic
    eruption, mudslide,
girl cliques in the corridor,
a muscle car and *his cheatin' heart*,
oh—*a poodle*

 Mark Twain ▮▮▮▮▮▮▮▮▮▮▮▮▮▮▮▮▮
▮▮▮▮▮▮▮▮▮▮▮▮▮▮▮▮▮▮ kept ▮ a barrel and fed
▮▮▮▮▮▮▮▮▮▮▮▮▮▮▮▮▮▮▮▮▮▮▮▮▮▮▮▮▮▮
▮▮▮▮▮▮▮▮▮ the bung hole.

The husband got himself over one
and since language evolves—

unlike a man's furtive activities—there was

email trash, bathroom trash, she-trash.
Which is to say, bung-trash.

Tense?

In a baby ████████████████████████████████████
███
███
████████████████ wiring ████ allows ██████████
████████████████████████████████████
██████████████████████████████████ wiring

From a lumpy pullout in our front room
that faced car alarms, hookers calling up to the neighbor

to buzz-me-in-baby, dawn-breaking garbage trucks,
and a boom box in the busted-up park—

I also knew a thumping in the far room:

our infant on her back in the crib
banging her feet on her mattress, realizing

just who jiggled the zebras circling
above her face, a beatific lightbulb.

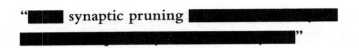
" ▮▮ synaptic pruning ▮▮▮▮▮▮▮▮▮▮
▮▮▮▮▮▮▮▮▮▮▮▮▮▮▮▮▮▮▮▮▮ "

Special shears to clip and shape. Save
and slip a twig into a vase

out of direct sun. Out of direct sunset
when father sent the girl to her room

saying,
You just ruined my supper.

Oh what power for a kindergartener—

this huge surge

is

a kind of

host

Waves sweep under the house pilings,

shoving sand and debris, scumming with salty grit.
Each night, the husband's erratic blood

pumps rivalry into his rib cage. A short-lived glacier,
I'm told. A spike in her fever. In voltage as well—

you know, that need to protect wires

from thunderbolt
striking across school yard then marriage

then one's child's childhood.
Warring factions. Tribes. Bring the soldiers home.

Home is where the surge is.

Resilience

A single drop of rain can weigh
fifty times as much as a mosquito and yet

the insect flies through a downpour without injury.

Rather than resist the impact, they
"go with the flow"—

like a boyfriend who trained in aikido—
and when there's a direct hit

the long wings and legs act "like a kite with a lengthy
    tail"

so the insect can pull through the globule
before it splats on the ground. Moreover,

when such resilience is used as a model for robots

we learn: "If you make it very, very small,
you basically don't have to do anything else

to make it survive." A tough exoskeleton helps.
Also a happy-go-lucky heart even though

his mother was strangled when he was seven.

Black Kite, White Plastic

You might consider plastic a convenience, a waste, or
deferred payment.

For black kites, white plastic is vital decor

indicating the resident, a superior strategist.
Before plastic? Perhaps cloth or paper. Before these?

"Maybe brightly colored feathers of other birds,
the white wool of sheep or deer . . .

or perhaps the behavior evolved after
such materials became available," offers an ornithologist.

Only the right amount of white plastic—not green or
      transparent—

serves as warning to those threatening foreclosure.
I reconsider our pugnacious white lawn chair in wonder.

circle

Circling a Sphere

When shut, an eye sees itself: planet, orbit,

a star, an egg, a raindrop before descent—
oh, and Prospect Park carousel.

That *ring around the rosie.* That gold ring

years before nipple ornament. Yes,
when shut, the eye discovers an oval table,

where conversing includes all angles
because "the shape of any object

represents the balance of two opposing forces."
A table where, with revolutionary cohorts,

speaking up was requisite

unlike family meals—the silenced
tablecloth, reticent bowls, mute plates.

The platter of bratwurst.

Oh, and Dr. Leibovitch noted:
"When you cook a frankfurter,

it always splits in the long direction:
because the sphere is tough." Tough, yes.

And Kandinsky added
that the circle is the most modest form

but asserts itself without condition. Therefore,
it's pivotal to challenge the family circle
with a round of verbal ammunition.

Circling a Nest

"The shapes of body parts
are assumed to have some relation to their purpose"

including the human egg—though bird eggs
are not round (as in a child's drawing)

which biologists attribute
"to both the arduous passage

the egg makes through the avian oviduct
and the fact that oval eggs

roll in a circle rather than a straight line
and thus are less likely to fall from a nest."

Both my daughters had to be wrenched out—
caesarean and forceps, respectively—

which affected their shapes (yes really)

and surely their temperaments.
Who knows of my own emergence

since my mother was innately circuitous.

For Nicole

Encircling a Snail

She stowed three hundred in her purse.
She loved to watch them conjugate.

Probably preferred fooling around with clothes wholly on.

Balls

Prince and coach. Coach and batter.

Cookie dough. Clay. Stick.
Bearings. Gum. Spit.

Have one—
but know: apart from nature

a sphere may indicate "human artifacture,"

a mark of handiwork.
Mandala, lotus throne, rose window. Wax.

Hula hoop mimics halo
while in his sleep my husband dodges so often

my head keeps spinning.

(Then there's Miss Molly
and what she sure likes best of all—)

The Compass

School supplies from the five-and-dime notwithstanding,
Donne's *stiff* compass

encompasses a forbidden *morning*
between getting loopy and

waking in the college rotunda.

I blamed his alchemy.

Circling an Eye

A professor of chaos theory

suggests that the eye's "most salient feature"
is the ball-thing. But if so, why?

To aid in focusing
(though "the whole spherical casing seems superfluous

to the optical need of that [fovea centralis]"
since the retina occupies so minute a pit)

or to enable the eye to roll in its socket

(though animals with fixed eyes
possess eyeballs as well)? My hunch

has less to do with the optical globe or chaos

and more with my husband's upward displacement
     anxiety
and down low eyeballing.

The Dream of a Raindrop

Whether tear or rain, neither appear round
on search engine images

even though scientifically speaking
the latter begins as a liquid globe—

"aggregates of water molecules
that have condensed around specks of dust or salt"—

until gravity has its way
and circle turns into chandelier-crystal:

drizzle, downpour, tempest.
Come inside Kimi, before you catch your death.

The Dream of Toast

Burnt before pop. Burnt before
black. Burnt before taste of charcoal.

Burnt before. Before firecrackers at the public pool
and sparklers stuck into sand

on my seventh birthday with as many candles.
Before, too, the breakfast table—

because dreams are merely "a physiological warm-up"
before one wakes up—

I digest whatever alarm is set on the counter
because I've gotten burned before

(not like men in a circle jerk—)
Before weed, champagne, or the Buttered Cat Paradox.

Before computer failure. Before a dedicated street
    murder.

Circles and Breasts

"A fertility signal, a youth signal, a health signal, a
    wealth symbol."
A gland and a store of fat.

"Mama" or, "¡Oye mamita!" if looking for a steamy
    date.
Preferably with real tissue.

For myself, born in the fifties: pillow and/or punishment.
For myself, struggling against the cliché of gravity.

For the Amazon, cutting off the right side

in order to shoot her arrow
                    straight into the adversary.

Frank?

"In the Middle Ages," Dr. Roy Gulick said,
"corpses of people who died of plague

were used as biological weapons
by catapulting them into walled cities."

This infected townspeople and catapulters alike
though it's unclear whether the disease spread

by bodily secretions or fleas. Why
Frank from Valhalla, NY

would ask a news blogger
if one could contract plague from a corpse—I can only
    imagine.

Plagued

Fleas largely transmitted
the zoonotic Black Death

unless of course a person had contact

with sordid tissue or bodily secretion.
Feeling plagued by her husband,

secretion brought to mind *secret* and *fluid*.
He'd just revealed *who, when, how often*—

every lousy detail except for *where*
and though none pertained to their holy matrimony

she couldn't shake the particulars.

Apart from debridement
she wasn't sure how to treat such extremity.

The Top Hit

*Now that we have taken the lid off these cells we see that
they are pumping out all this transcriptional energy.*
—DAVID F. CLAYTON, SONGBIRD BIOLOGIST

The indigo bunting's changeable love song

contrasts with the zebra finch's single version
because, though the latter is capable of a larger
   repertoire,

the cells control the song.

So, where we might have blamed surroundings
for sensational limitation *or* variation

now we can see that genome findings
on the mechanism for vocal learning

have undercut the common view of the brain
as relatively stable—which is to say

my husband's multifarious come-ons

were hardly scripted on trains where doo-wop was
   rehearsed
but from patriarchs on the Grand Concourse.

For Harold

conveying *love*

". . . the brain is constantly rewiring itself based on daily life. In the end, what we pay the most attention to defines us."

Stuck smacks of "duck" or masking tape. Mud, tar, quicksand, and besotted. Then again, *vortex* stirs up whirlpool, drain, and dump. All ways of opposites. Always mulling over muck. His. His?

"Thanks to advances in neuroimaging, we now have evidence that a baby's first attachments imprint its brain."

Ah, ah, ah. Blank. Long black hair. Blanket. Blank. Hands handling. Blank. Blank. Cotton. Cotton is *mamama.* Cotton blanket is blankety-blank.

She keeps that number in "contacts" so she knows when to connect, or not.

"It isn't that caregiving changes genes; it influences how the genes express themselves as the child grows."

I don't want her beat-up Tiny Tears . . . I don't want her stinky skort . . . I won't go to her Sweet Sixteen . . . I don't want to hear his ex's name, any of their names . . . I do want to teach someone a lesson . . .

The Dream of Shells, Cocoons, Pods, and Even Husks

Ah, giant turtle nearly extinct!
Ah, caterpillars in the evergreens we had to fumigate!

Ah, what we pick to devour each night!

The scientist said, "You are seeing the split-brain in
    action"

because one side is partially conscious even in sleep.

Ah—and never return out of loneliness
especially to the bitter mattress!

"Breaking old habits isn't easy, since habits are deeply ingrained neural shortcuts, a way of slurring over details without having to dwell on them."

Shortcuts? Like to grandmother's?

or

When he saw his daughter's new haircut, by way of a greeting he said, "Did you read in the news that a lesbian was raped in Prospect Park?"

or

slurring or *slur?*

or

Tweezing, etc.

or

When she saw crumbs on the passenger seat, she assumed he was cheating on her with an ex or with a babysitter or neighbor or adjunct or manicurist—

or

She *smelled a rat*—

"Dr. Siegel, a neuropsychiatrist, refers to the indelible sense of 'feeling felt' that we learn as infants and seek in romantic love, a reciprocity that remodels the brain's architecture and functions."

Oh, envy the dove the dovecote!

"Wedded hearts change everything, even the brain."

She asked the mirror, *who is fairest in the land?* and the mirror declared, *the daughter of your husband.* So she instructed a huntsman to cut out the girl's heart, though in the end he brought her that of a wild boar. Though at heart she did not cease that instruction.

". . . we learn as infants and seek in romantic love, a reciprocity that remodels the brain's architecture and functions."

Oh, envy the tree the treehouse!

Things That Make One's Stomach Churn

AFTER SEI SHŌNAGON

The guinea worm back in the news.

His old photo album. His laptop and the word "lap."

Tripe.

A dirty kitchen sink. This is where one washes dishes
and rinses vegetables! Even the empty sink is gray with
grime, whether porcelain or metal. The faucet handles as
well. (How *does* he get toothpaste on the spout?)

The pigeon cooing every morning under the air
conditioner that we never bother to remove. She will not
scare away. Almost as troubling as a four-star restaurant
full of children.

Files—goes without saying. I mean, *flies*.

His files.

Erasing "The Aging Brain"

jiggle

                         bump

      hang around

                wrestle

                              tune

            push and

work

        the   egg

                    keep

disorienting

that

scramble

Erasing "Host Manipulation"

Not all   kill their hosts

                                         Think of the morgue

Providing room and board

some   migrate to their host's brain

       distressing to those committed to "autonomy," but   the

               invaders

ask

who benefits when people

sleep when tired, scratch an itch or write a poem

Buddhists note

I don't know about the pineapple or the yellow, but
absorbent and porous are we

Brain Implant #3: Patterns

Though still a long way from being tested in humans,
the implant demonstrates for the first time that a cognitive
function can be improved with a device that mimics the firing
patterns of neurons.

—BENEDICT CAREY

Karl von Frisch related his study of "dance language" to
  bee communication
SAT bubbles
An anxiety disorder characterized by intrusive thoughts that
  produce uneasiness, apprehension, fear, or worry, by
  repetitive behaviors . . . [Symptoms] can be alienating and
  time consuming . . . (Wikipedia)
From the French, *patron*
McCall's catalogs in Home Ec.
She splits her split ends. She pulls each blind down
  exactly halfway. She checks his in-box. She reads the
  Airline Safety Instruction card before takeoff.
Penrose, Pongal, Kolam, Fractal, Fern
Infidelities
She eats dryer sheets.
M.O.

Sudoku

"Each individual has a pattern integrity," R. Buckminster
Fuller

The cold front forms in the wake of an extratropical
cyclone.

fluctuation (Antonym)

The Problem with Dwarfs

Astronomers have severely undercounted
the stars in the universe partly due to dwarf stars

in "bobbly and elliptical" galaxies.
K. Chang describes the latest technique

to count things one cannot see:

"Because the dwarfs are cooler,
the fingerprint of certain colors they emit and absorb

is different from that of larger stars." The numbers
    matter
in studying how galaxies formed and grew over eons.

My view on dwarf stars involves my mother-in-law
who, before I married her son, described my height as
    such

to dissuade him from marrying me (or anyone). No
    matter
that others considered me a kind of star—adjuncting at
    an Ivy—

or that large women resemble bobbly transvestites
which I didn't say since I tend to keep my little mouth
   shut,

making my opinions known, elliptically. In any case,
compared to giants, dwarfs are cooler.

Cherry Stems

I'm not too happy that fruit flies have brains

since I swat them whenever I see them or think I see
        them.
I know about their brains because I met a scientist

who tinkers with their "learning circuitry,"
"the actual mechanics

of how a memory trace is laid down in a nerve cell or
        neuron."

All this proxy—dissecting the behavior of an insect—
to figure out how the brain works

for something like typing at which my mother was a pro

and me, fairly miserable because of some disorder
which it seems my daughter has inherited

since she also exhibits left/right confusion. However,

she can twist a cherry stem into a bow with her tongue
an ability no doubt from an ancestral brain

but which also reveals something about a summer in
    Florence.
In other words, too-much-information regarding
    memory trace.

For Miyako and Reiko

The Morphology of Flowers

Even Darwin saw the evolution of flowers as "an
    abominable mystery"

and in current experiments on "ancient appendage-
    building genes"
a scientist reasserts that "mutations set off grotesque
    changes"—

that is, things grow where they do not belong.
Thus, the petals of water lilies are not in and of
    themselves

"radical or mysterious." What is radical *and* mysterious

is the evolution of fancy as she dusts off fossil fragments
to examine an early impression:

small, rare, and growing in the shadow of the then more
    successful.
Distant cousin to the pine. Daughter-in-law of the star
    anise.

Concubine of the ginkgo.

memory

erasing *The Biology of Memory*

1.

        Unconscious
House
            edited

by   neighbors. No one spoke to me in school
                 anymore   roughed up
                    looted
out.

2.

in the terror quota when
Ludwig made the crossing alone

how unfrightened I was

3.

      Fritz

was drawn to
         everything   from schizophrenia to ingrown
toenails

       in   case
    shame
                    never became a

science.

4.

one at a time

a hippocampus nerve cell
communicates with other cells   named Brenda

but alas, that didn't give insight

5.

We discovered

in the snail

that

enhancing

trauma

is

in the end   who we are. We're all

horrible   shapes

For Matthea and Rob

The Dream of Leaves

How to access the material
of the unborn or the infant dream?

To rate, say, a rustling?

To value leaves rustling
before one realizes *leaves*? Before

one knows what a homonym is
or that every one thing

is a homonym after crowning—

Luminous Vapours

ORIGINALLY WRITTEN FOR *THE AMERICAN POETRY REVIEW*

A quibble [i.e., pun] is to Shakespeare what luminous vapours are to the traveller! He follows it to all adventures; it is sure to lead him out of his way, sure to engulf him in the mire. It has some malignant power over his mind, and its fascinations are irresistible.

—SAMUEL JOHNSON

"A Dream of Toast" may appear to have nothing in common with Japanese poetics but "toast" is where my abiding interest in Japanese aesthetics has led me.

Over the years I have cultivated my use of word associations, erratic repetition, and lists. An early influence came from Ivan Morris's translation of *The Pillow Book of Sei Shōnagon* where an artful catalog is elegant writing. In a list format, variation to repetition keeps things moving—*moving* as in pace and emotion. One variation comes up when a word shifts in meaning. This variation can add a new dimension to the list. For the "Dream of" series, I gave myself an assignment:

repeat a phrase, use a quote (specifically from an article on dream theory), hold the number of lines under twenty.

In "A Dream of Toast," I began with the word "toast" to see how far the homonyms would take me: bread browned by heat (especially the smell and taste), being burnt, the raising of glasses to honor someone, a "warm body," to be in a non-functioning state, and slang for a homicide victim. I wanted "toast" to be a portal from one meaning to the next.

Of course, paranomasia is not uncommon in the West, especially in the form of pun and double entendre. In comparison, because Japanese is vocabulary-poor, it is especially rich in words with multiple meanings. Wordplay is so deeply appreciated that there are at least three poetic terms for it. Robert Brower and Earl Miner describe them in *Japanese Court Poetry*: *engo* ("word association," i.e., *a word that has or creates an association with the preceding word or situation, often bringing out an additional dimension*), *honkadori* ("allusive variation," which can be compared to literary allusion, is specifically *the echoing of the words . . . of a well-known earlier poem in such a way that recognizable elements are incorporated into a new meaning . . .*).

The third is *kakekotoba*, "pivot-word." In revising work, recent and previous, I have often chosen a word that suggests several meanings in an attempt to burst out of a linear experience. The word can shift the progression. Brower and Miner's definition of *kakekotoba*: *a rhetorical scheme of wordplay in which a series of sounds is so employed as to mean two or more things at once by different parsings.*

Also valued in Japanese aesthetics is asymmetry, as in the odd number of syllables in both tanka and haiku. I've continued my preference for one- and two-lined stanzas to create an offbeat effect. Also for the sake of placement—as well as a spontaneous quality—I favor an erratic pattern of slant rhyme.

Naturally, I have also absorbed the use of innuendo from Western culture, whether Shakespeare or Mae West. And Dickinson's slant rhyme and eccentric use of dashes absolutely arousing. And repetition can be inspiring, as in incantation. I hope that my set of quirky lyric poems conveys a passion for such variables.

Notes

Epigraph
"Things That Make One's Stomach Churn," Sei Shōnagon, translated by Kimiko Hahn.

"[Kimiko's Clipping Morgue]"
Quote in *BRAIN fever* line is from Wikipedia. Also see "Brain Fever," "*Q&A*," C. Claiborne Ray, *NYT*, May 24, 1994.

CONSCIOUSNESS series
The consciousness poems throughout were triggered by lines from "The Riddle of Consciousness," Benedict Carey, *NYT*, February 7, 2010. The triggering quotes that do not appear as epigraphs are:
"Wake"
You know the person is there, you just don't know how much is still there." Or know what's there relates to what we call waking consciousness.

"Figure"
[The search] for the essence of consciousness all started with a simple presumption: Consciousness must begin where unconsciousness ends.

"Porch Light"
Theologians have likened this state of pre-awakening to sleep, to darkness, to life underground.

"Skull"
After five years of being in effect buried alive in its own skull, what kind of consciousness was left for this patient?

"Tiny Wheels"
So far, the precise neural correlates of consciousness—the brain circuits critical to "turning on" conscious awareness—have eluded capture.

"A Bowl of Spaghetti"
"In Pursuit of a Mind Map, Slice by Slice," Ashlee Vance, *NYT,* December 27, 2010

"Turns of Mind"
"Mass Animal Deaths: An Environmental Whodunit," James Gorman, *NYT,* January 8, 2011

DREAM series
With the exception of "The Dream of a Raindrop," all the dream poems were triggered by "A Dream Interpretation: Tuneups for the Brain," Benedict Carey, *NYT,* November 10, 2009.

Also "The Dream of a Letter Opener in the Shape of a Mermaid" contains a reference to the so-called Feejee Mermaid, popularized by P. T. Barnum.

"The Terrible-Headed-Lizard-from-the-Orient" [formerly "Ode to the Straw"]
"Paleontologists Put Ancient Long-Necked Monster in Its

Place," John Noble Wilford, *NYT*, September 28, 2004 (Note that "two hundred million years" is off by an additional thirty.)

"Ode to Home"
"In Snails and Snakes, Features to Delight Darwin," Sean B. Carroll, *NYT*, November 23, 2009

TIME series
The quotes at the head of each poem are titles, not epigraphs, and from: "Where Did Time Go? Do Not Ask the Brain Where Time Went," Benedict Carey *NYT*, January 5, 2010.

"The Solitary Adelie"
"As Winter Nears, Leaving the Ice," Jeff Vervoort and John Goodge, *NYT*, January 20, 2011

"The Secret Lives of Planets"
Lines more or less lifted from "Now in Sight: Far-Off Planets," Dennis Overbye, *NYT*, Nov. 14, 2008

PUZZLE series as follows:
"Giraffes"
"Tracing the Spark of Creative Problem-Solving," Benedict Carey, *NYT,* December 6, 2010

"Fiero"
"On a Hunt for What Makes Gamers Keep Gaming," John Tierney, *NYT*, December 6, 2010. Quote is edited.

"Riddle"
"Tracing the Spark of Creative Problem-Solving," Benedict Carey, *NYT*, December 6, 2010

"Mapping"
"In Pursuit of a Mind Map, Slice by Slice," Ashlee Vance, *NYT*, December 27, 2010

"Madagascan Hissing Cockroaches"
"Not Too Large, Not Too Small, but Spoiling for a Fight," Sindya N. Bhanoo, *NYT*, December 22, 2010

THE TEENAGE BRAIN series
"Inside the Teenage Brain," Judith Newman, *Parade*, November 28, 2010. My titles from the following quotes:
"Dopamine"
"Without adequate levels [of dopamine], life can be a disaster. It's like: I'm crossing the street. There's a truck approaching me and . . . oh, look at the cute doggy!"

"Mark Twain . . ."
"the Mark Twain approach to child-rearing: 'When a child turns 12, he should be kept in a barrel and fed through the bung hole, until he reaches 16 . . . at which time you plug the bung hole.'"

"In a baby . . ."
"In a baby, each neuron (a cell that transmits electric signals) has around 2500 synapses . . . These synapses are the wiring that allows our brains to send and receive information. Until recently, scientists thought this huge surge in brain wiring . . ." (J. Shatkin)

"synaptic pruning . . ."
"This synaptic pruning in a sense makes you become the
person you'll ultimately be." (J. Shatkin)

"this huge surge . . ."
"this huge surge in brain wiring happened only once,
when kids are young. Wrong. A study of 145 kids and
adolescents scanned every two years at the NIH has shown
that there is another huge surge right before adolescence,
followed by a process of 'pruning' those connections in
a kind of use-it-or-lose-it strategy. In other words, says
Jess Shatkin, assistant professor of child and adolescent
psychiatry and pediatrics at the NYU Child Study
Center and host"

"Resilience"
"For Mosquitoes, Rain Isn't a Flight Hazard," Sindya N.
Bhanoo, *NYT*, June 5, 2012

"Black Kite, White Plastic"
"Feathering Their Nests With Plastic, and Getting Ahead,"
Sindya N. Bhanoo, *NYT*, January 20, 2011

CIRCLE series
Triggered by Natalie Angier's "The Circular Logic of
the Universe," *NYT*, December 8, 2009. Note that the
Kandinsky quote has been altered from: the circle "is the
most perfect form, but asserts itself unconditionally."

"Frank?" and "Plagued"
"Can You Contract Plague From a Corpse?," "Q&A,"
C. Claiborne Ray, *NYT*, June 5, 2012

"The Top Hit"
"The Top Hit" uses material from "From a Songbird, New Insights Into the Brain," Nicholas Wade, *NYT*, April 5, 2010 and
"For Some Birds, It's Not Always the Same Old Song," Henry Fountain, *NYT*, April 19, 2010

CONVEYING *LOVE* series
For the titles I've used quotes—with apologies—from "The Brain on Love," Diane Ackerman, *NYT*, March 24, 2012

"Erasing 'The Aging Brain'"
"How to Train the Aging Brain," Barbara Strauch, *NYT*, January 3, 2010

"Erasing 'Host Manipulation'"
"Who's in Charge Inside Your Head?" by David P. Barash, *NYT*, October 6, 2012

"The Problem with Dwarfs"
"How Many Stars? Three Times as Many as We Thought, Report Says," Kenneth Chang, *NYT*, December 1, 2010

"Cherry Stems"
"Researchers Create Artificial Memories in the Brain of a Fruitfly," Nicholas Wade, *NYT*, October 19, 2009

"The Morphology of Flowers"
"Where Did All the Flowers Come From?," Carl Zimmer, *NYT*, September 7, 2009

MEMORY sequence
"A Quest to Understand How Memory Works," Claudia
Dreifus, *NYT*, March 5, 2012

"Luminous Vapours"
This essay—originally titled "A Dream of Toast"—was
written for "The Poet on the Poem," *The American Poetry
Review.*

Acknowledgments

A heartfelt thanks to those writers who do not even know how thoroughly I admire their work: the *New York Times* science writers. Personal thanks to Jacqueline Phung for safeness; to Nicole Cooley, Anne Marie Macari, and Roger Sedarat for their keen notes on my drafts; and to Jill Bialosky, from whom I continue to learn how to make some order.

A loving thanks to the remarkable young women in my life— Reiko, Miyako, Laura, Elizabeth. And to Harold, long-suffering hero of numerous poems—especially given my many acts of poetic license.

Finally, sincere thanks to the Guggenheim Memorial Foundation for the fellowship that arrived just as I was beginning to wonder: after *Toxic Flora* what next?

Acceptance from the editors of these journals has meant much to me—in particular, David Bonanno, Brett Fletcher Lauer, David Lynn, and Michael Waters.

The American Poetry Review (2011)
"The Poet on the Poem"
"A Dream of Bubbles"
"A Dream of Knife, Fork, and Spoon"
"A Dream of Yellow Leaves"

"A Dream of Shells, Cocoons, Pods, and Even Husks"
"A Dream of Toast"
"A Dream of a Letter Opener in the Shape of a Mermaid"
"After five years of . . ."
" 'You know the person is there . . ."
"Before doctors learn . . ."
"[The search] for the essence of consciousness . . ."
"So far, the precise neural correlates . . ."
"Cherry Stems"
"The Morphology of Flowers"

The American Poetry Review (2013)
"Circling a Sphere"
"Balls"
"The Compass"
"Circling an Eye"
"The Dream of a Raindrop"
"Mark Twain . . ."
"Pruning . . ."
"this huge surge . . ."

Believer
"Black Kite, White Plastic"

Black Renaissance Noire
"Ode to the Terrible-Headed-Lizard-from-the-Orient" [formerly
    "Ode to the Straw"]

Drunken Boat (online journal)
"A French explorer . . ."

"[Some psychologists say] the findings support . . ."
"But the way [the brain] . . ."
"Yet the sensation of passing time . . ."
"By contrast, the new research suggests . . ."

Everyday Genius
"The What-Have-You"

failbetter (online)
"conveying *love*" sequence

FIELD
"A Dream of Parsnips"
"A Dream of a Pillow"

Granta
"Madagascan Hissing Cockroaches"

Great River Review
"Frank?"
"Plagued"

H_NGM_N
Things That Make One's Stomach Churn
"The Problem with Dwarfs"
"Mapping"
"Fiero"

Hanging Loose
"Riddle #1"

jubilat
"erasing *The Biology of Memory*"

The Kenyon Review
"Circling the Nest"

KR (online)
"Circles and Breasts"

The Margins
"The Dream of a Little Occupied Japan Doll"
"The Dream of *Shōji*"
"Resilience"

The Minnesota Review/Virginia Tech
"The Solitary Adelie"
"Ode to Home"

Plume (online journal)
"'People have a hard time understanding . . .'"
". . . [S]cientists are not sure . . ."
"In earlier work, researchers found . . ."
"Left to its own devices . . ."
"[Kimiko's Clipping Morgue]"

Poem-A-Day, Academy of American Poets
"Giraffes"

Poetry
"The Dream of a Lacquer Box"
"The Dream of a Fire Engine"
"A Bowl of Spaghetti"

A Public Space
"Gag"
"Porch Light"

Storyscape
"Turns of Mind"
"The Top Hit"
"Brain Implant #3: Patterns"

Tongue
"Erasing 'Host Manipulation'"
"The Secret Lives of Planets"